507
MIL

MILGROM, Harry

First Experiments with Gravity

727

First Experiments with Gravity

FIRST EXPERIMENTS WITH

Illustrated by Lewis Zacks

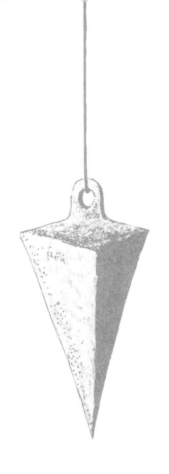

GRAVITY

Harry Milgrom

E. P. DUTTON & CO., INC. - New York

Fourth Printing August 1968

Materials

All the materials for the experiments in this book are easy to obtain. The following list is a guide to the kind, size, and shape of materials needed.

Through space research, scientists will soon free man from the earth to journey to other planets. Someday you, dear reader, may be among the scientists who will free man from the evils of war, starvation, and disease that still afflict the human race.

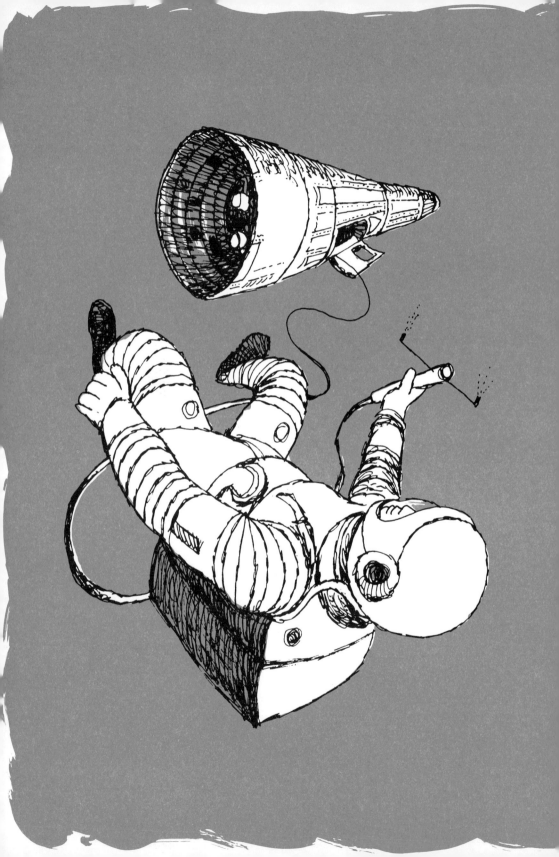

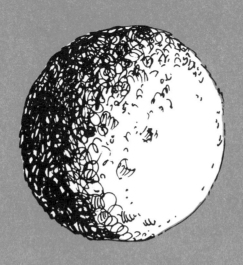

Imagine that you are an astronaut. You are seated
in your capsule, waiting for the countdown to be completed.
You hear the final count, and the rocket blasts off. As the
rocket steadily picks up speed, you move higher and higher
above the earth. Then the last stage of the rocket puts your
spaceship into orbit. It whirls around the earth once every
90 minutes at the fantastic speed of 18,000 miles per hour.

As soon as you are in orbit, you are weightless. If you stood
on a scale, the pointer would remain at zero. Everything in
the ship is weightless. The capsule itself is weightless. What
can make an object lose its weight?

In order to answer that question, you need to know what weight is. More than three hundred years ago, Sir Isaac Newton, the famous British scientist, figured out how to explain the weight of things. He noticed that when an apple breaks off a tree, it always drops to the ground. As a result, he reasoned that the apple falls because the earth attracts it. This led him to the big idea that matter is attracted to matter by a mysterious force. He named it the *force of gravity*. The weight of an object on earth is a measure of the force of gravity between the matter in the object and the matter in the earth.

Now, let's see what can make things become weightless. If the earth's gravity suddenly stopped tugging, then everything at or near its surface would lose all weight. With a slight push of your foot against the ground you could send yourself out into space. You would not be able to pour water from a pitcher into a glass. All objects would have to be fastened to the ground to keep them from leaving the earth.

An object becomes weightless when the earth's force of gravity on the object is balanced by an equal force in the opposite direction. This happens when a capsule is in orbit around the earth. The whirling motion pulls the capsule away from the earth. This balances the earth's gravity, which pulls the capsule toward the earth, and everything in the capsule, including the astronaut, becomes weightless.

As a spaceship travels away from the earth, the earth's force of gravity becomes weaker and weaker. If you weigh 100 pounds on earth, you would weigh 25 pounds 4,000 miles out in space. You would weigh only 1 pound if you were 36,000 miles from the earth. Should a spaceship travel far enough away, the ship and everything in it would be weightless.

If a spaceship lands on the moon, or on one of the other planets of our solar system, its occupants will then have weight again. However, their weight will not be the same as on earth. Since the moon and the planets are smaller or larger than the earth, each one has a different force of gravity. If you weigh 100 pounds on the earth, here is what you would weigh on the moon and the planets:

on	you would weigh	on	you would weigh
The moon	16 pounds	Jupiter	265 pounds
Mercury	38 pounds	Saturn	117 pounds
Venus	87 pounds	Uranus	105 pounds
Mars	39 pounds	Neptune	123 pounds
		Pluto	50 pounds

In the future, spacemen will have to deal with the force of gravity wherever they travel in the universe. That is why astronauts are being trained to function under conditions where there is no weight. Should their destination in space have more or less matter than the earth, the astronauts will also need to know how to move about and work when their bodies and equipment are heavier or lighter than on earth.

Sir Isaac Newton's explanation of weight had its beginning as he watched an apple fall from a tree. He wasn't satisfied to know simply that apples fall to the ground; he wanted to know why this happened.

The experiments in this book will help you to explore the force of gravity. Perform these experiments carefully. Watch everything that takes place, and think about what each experiment means.

Someday, when you get to know much more about gravity, you will discover new ways of using and controlling the effects of this strange force.

1 Before you start to explore the earth's gravity, find out what you have to do to make something move.

Place a book on a long strip of wrapping paper on a table. Does the book move by itself? No, it does not; but it does move when you push it with your finger or pull it with the paper. Try the same thing with other objects. In each case, the object remains at rest until you push it or pull it.

The word *force* is another name for a push or a pull. Therefore, you can be sure that whenever an object begins to move, a force is acting upon it.

Now, hold a baseball in your hand at eye level. Let go of the ball. What happens to it? It begins to move toward the ground. This means that a force must be acting on the ball. Try the same thing with other kinds of balls. Each time, the ball starts to fall when you let go of it. Each time, the earth's pull of gravity is the force that makes the ball move.

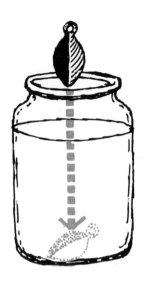

 Now, here is a puzzle. You know that the earth's gravity acts on all things. Why, then, do they not all fall to the ground?

Put a lead sinker in the palm of your right hand. Gravity pulls the weight in one direction. What does your hand do to it? Your hand pushes the weight in the opposite direction. As long as the pull of gravity and the push of your hand balance each other, the sinker does not move.

Put the lead sinker on a table. Gravity pulls the weight in one direction. The table pushes against the weight in the opposite direction. In this case, also, the weight does not move so long as the pull of gravity and the push of the table balance each other.

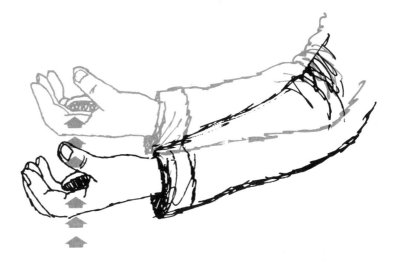

Fill a large jar with water. Put the lead sinker on the water. What happens to the weight? It moves to the bottom of the jar.

Gravity pulls the weight in one direction. The liquid water cannot balance the pull of gravity the way the solid table does, so the weight moves in the direction of the bigger force, the pull of gravity.

Put the lead sinker in the palm of your hand again. This time, raise your hand. What happens to the weight? It moves with your hand. In this case, the push of your hand is greater than the pull of gravity. So the weight moves in the direction of the bigger force, the push of your hand.

The answer to this puzzle is simple. Whenever the pull of gravity on an object is balanced by an opposite force, the object does not move. If the pull of gravity is greater than the opposite force, the object falls. If the opposite force is greater than the pull of gravity, the object moves up.

15

3 Which object does gravity pull to the ground faster, a light one or a heavy one?

You will need the help of another person to find the answer to this question. Have him hold a rubber ball (the light object) in his left hand and a baseball (the heavy object) in his right hand. Ask him to hold both balls at eye level. On the floor, under the balls, put down a large piece of cardboard or other material to protect the floor.

Tell the person holding the balls to let go when you say "Go." Make sure that you can see the balls when they reach the floor. Give the signal. When do the balls hit the floor? Both balls get to the floor at the same time. In other words, gravity pulls the light ball to the ground just as fast as it pulls the heavy one.

Do the same experiment with other pairs of objects. Use a dime and a quarter, a large nail and a pencil of the same size, or a sponge and a block of wood of the same size.

In each case, the two objects reach the floor at the same time. These experiments show that most objects move to the ground at the same speed when dropped from the same height. This is true when gravity is the main force that acts on the objects.

4 A falling weight can move other things.

Attach a small wagon to the end of a 4-foot string. Attach the lead sinker to the other end of the string.

Place the wagon at one end of a table. Let the weight hang over an edge at the other end. What happens to the wagon when you release the weight?

The falling weight moves the wagon. Try the same thing again. This time put a heavy object, such as a book, on the wagon. If the wagon moves at all, it does so more slowly than before.

Falling weights are usually used in grandfather clocks to move the gears that turn the hands of the clocks.

When certain objects drop, another force becomes important enough to change the speed of fall.

Let's investigate this force. On a piece of paper draw the outline of a quarter, and cut out the paper circle with scissors. Repeat the steps in experiment 3, using the paper circle and the quarter.

What happens when the two objects are released? The quarter moves to the floor quickly. But the paper circle takes much longer to fall. What do you think makes the difference?

Both the paper and the quarter move through air as they fall. The air pushes against each object. The push of the air against the coin is small compared to the coin's weight (the force of gravity). As a result, the air hardly slows up the coin. But the push of the air against the paper is almost as much as the paper's weight (the force of gravity). As a result, the air slows up the paper much more than it does the coin, and the coin reaches the floor before the paper does.

The force of the air against an object is called *air resistance*. Air resistance against a small object is small. Air resistance against a large object is large.

20

How can air resistance be used to slow the fall of a heavy object?

Make a paper parachute as shown in the diagram. Obtain two large iron washers. Attach one washer to the string of the parachute. Hold the top of the parachute in one hand and the second washer in the other hand. Make sure that both washers are at the same height.

Let go of the parachute and the single washer. Which washer reaches the floor last? The washer attached to the parachute hits the floor after the unattached one because air resistance against the large surface of the parachute slows up the fall of the attached washer.

You know, of course, that parachutes are used to lower things slowly from airplanes. In this way, people and packages can fall great distances and yet not be damaged when they strike the ground. Parachutes are also used to slow orbiting capsules when they reenter the earth's atmosphere.

7 In what other way can you slow the speed with which an object falls to the ground?

With a shoebox cover or a piece of cardboard make a hill. Place one washer at the top of the hill. Nearby, but not over the hill, hold the second washer at the same height as the first. Release both washers at once. What do you observe?

The washer on the hill slides slowly to the bottom. The second washer falls more quickly. The washer on the hill is slowed by two forces. First, the hill holds up a part of the washer's weight. Second, the washer rubbing against the cardboard results in a force of friction. This also holds up a part of the washer's weight.

Change the slant of the hill and repeat the experiment. What happens to the speed of fall as the hill is made steeper? What happens as the hill is made less steep? How does this explain why it is easier for a person to walk down a flight of steps than to walk down a hill?

How can you find out which way is down and which way is up?

Attach the lead sinker to a string about a foot long. Hold the free end of the string high enough to lift the weight off the table. Pull the weight to one side. What happens when you release it?

It swings back and forth over and over again and slowly comes to a stop. Each time the sinker ends up in the same place when it stops swinging.

When the sinker is at rest, the direction from the top of the string to the weight is down. If you could continue into the earth in this direction, you would pass near its center. Gravity, then, pulls toward the center of the earth. The direction from the sinker to the top of the string is up. If you could continue in this direction, you would move farther and farther away from the center of the earth.

The weight on a string is used by builders to make sure
that walls and doorways stand up straight. Test the walls
and doorways in your house in this way. Hold the top of the
string against the side of a door opening. If the weight just
touches the side, then it is standing up straight. If the weight
hangs far from the side, then it is slanted. When used for this
purpose, the weight is called a *plumb bob,* and the string is
called a *plumb line.*

 How can the force of gravity be used to measure time?

Tie one end of a 4-foot string to the lead sinker. Have someone hold the string at a distance of 20 inches from the sinker. Make sure that it can swing in any direction.

Push the weight to one side and then let go of it. What happens to the weight? Gravity pulls it down as far as the string will let it go. Then the weight moves up on the opposite side until it is stopped by gravity. It falls from the second side back to the first one. This is repeated over and over again. The sinker swings back and forth and slowly comes to a stop.

While the weight is swinging, shorten the string to 10 inches. What does this do to the movement of the weight?

28

It swings back and forth more quickly than at a distance of 20 inches.

Again, while the weight is swinging, let the string out to 39 inches. What does this do to the movement of the weight? It swings back and forth more slowly than at a distance of 20 inches.

A swinging weight is called a "pendulum." A long pendulum swings slowly. A short pendulum swings quickly.

Obtain a watch with a sweep second hand. Swing the weight on 10, 20, and 39 inches of string as before. In each case, count the number of times the weight moves back and forth in one minute. (One complete turn of the sweep second hand takes sixty seconds, or one minute.) Keep a record of your count.

Length of string	Number of swings in 1 minute
10 inches	
20 inches	
39 inches	

When the string is about 39 inches long, the weight moves back and forth 60 times in 1 minute. This pendulum makes a swing each second. As long as it keeps moving, it ticks off seconds. Now you know why an old-fashioned grandfather clock has a pendulum.

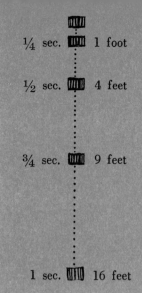

1/4 sec. 1 foot

1/2 sec. 4 feet

3/4 sec. 9 feet

1 sec. 16 feet

10 There is another way to measure time with the help of gravity.

An object that falls many feet takes more time to drop than one that falls a smaller distance. It takes an object 1 second to fall 16 feet; $\frac{3}{4}$ second to fall 9 feet; $\frac{1}{2}$ second to fall 4 feet; $\frac{1}{4}$ second to fall 1 foot.

Hold the rubber ball 4 feet above the floor. From the moment you let go of the ball until it hits the floor, the time is $\frac{1}{2}$ second. For a drop of 1 foot, the time is $\frac{1}{4}$ second. By dropping an object from heights of less than 16 feet, you can measure parts of a second.

If the height is more than 16 feet, then the time is more than 1 second. For example, it takes an object 2 seconds to fall 64 feet; 3 seconds to fall 144 feet; 4 seconds to fall 256 feet; 5 seconds to fall 400 feet.

To find the distance for any other number of seconds, multiply 4 by the number of seconds. Next, multiply the figure you get by itself. You will then have the distance.

30

The force of gravity gives an object its weight. How can you tell if one object weighs more than another?

Place the rubber ball in your hand. It feels light. Now, re-place the rubber ball with the baseball. The baseball feels heavy. Sometimes you can use your hand in this way to tell which of two objects is heavier. With your hand, however, you only guess or estimate the weights. To measure them accurately you need a scale.

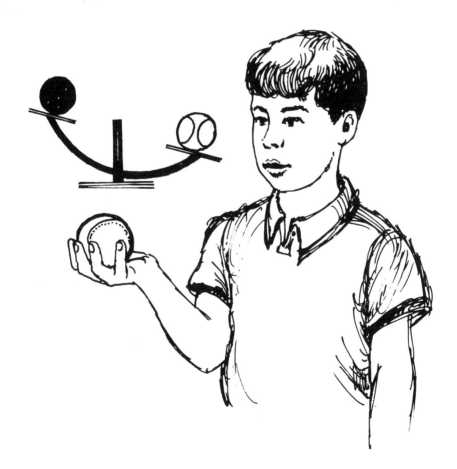

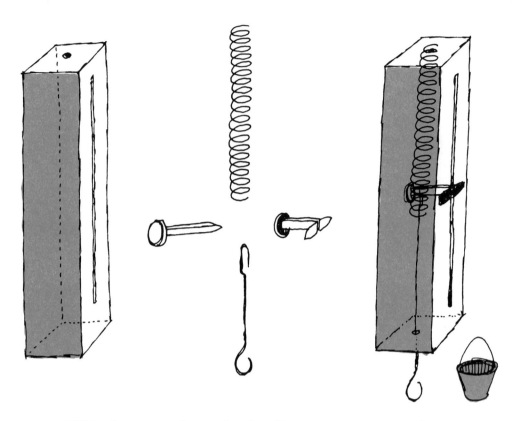

With the parts shown in the diagram, you can make a scale. Put the scale together as follows:

1. On the inside of the box at the top, attach one end of the spring.
2. Put the loop of the pointer through the slit in the box.
3. Push the free end of the spring through the pointer loop.
4. Slip the straight end of the long wire through the hole at the bottom of the box.
5. Bend the straight end of the wire into a U. Attach the U to the pointer loop.

Your scale is ready for use if the pointer moves away from the top as the wire hook is pulled out. Hang the little cup on the hook. With a pencil line, mark the position of the top edge of the pointer. Write the number *0* next to this line to show that it is the starting line.

Which is heavier, a quarter or a nickel?

Put a nickel in the cup. Draw a line to show the top edge of the pointer.

Put a quarter in the cup. What does the pointer show? The nickel and the quarter have about the same weight. If the quarter weighed more than the nickel, the pointer would move past the nickel mark. If the quarter weighed less than the nickel, the pointer would not reach the nickel mark.

Weight is shown by the stretch of the spring. The bigger the weight, the bigger the stretch. The smaller the weight, the smaller the stretch. Of course, the spring snaps back to the same place when the weight is taken off.

Compare the weights of coins, marbles, nails, screws, and other small objects. First, estimate which of two things is heavier. Second, use the scale to find out if your estimate is right. Keep a record of the results.

Pair of objects	Estimated weight	Scale weight
penny and nail	penny is heavier	

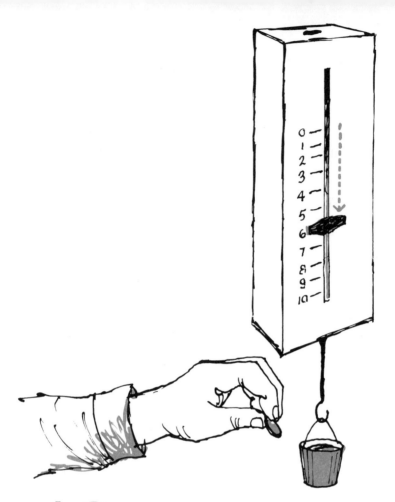

12 To get the weight of a single object, each line on your scale must represent a specific weight.

Here is one way to give each line on the scale some kind of number. Hang the cup on the scale. Put a penny in the cup. Draw a line to show the position of the top edge of the pointer. Mark this line *1*. Do the same thing with two pennies, three pennies, and so on up to ten pennies.

Now you know each line stands for a pennyweight. If an object stretches the spring so that the pointer goes to the sixth line past *0*, then the object weighs as much as six pennies.

Measure the weights of coins, marbles, and other things. Show the weights on a chart.

Object	*Pennyweights*
quarter	
marble	

In order to measure heavier weights, the scale must have a stiffer spring. If the lines are given numbers that stand for 1 ounce, 2 ounces, and so on, the scale weighs in ounces. If the lines are given numbers that stand for 1 pound, 2 pounds, and so on, the scale weighs in pounds. (There are 16 ounces in a pound.) Scales of this kind are called spring scales.

13

How can you tell which way is downhill?

If the hill is steep, you can see which way is downhill. But if the hill is not steep, you may not be able to tell. In such a case, you can use a ball to find out.

Put the rubber ball on a table. If the table is level, the ball will not roll one way or another.

Now, lift one end of the table. What happens to the ball? It rolls in the direction of downhill. The steeper the hill, the faster the ball rolls.

A disk (wheel) with a wide, flat rim can also be used instead of a ball. In the next experiment you will discover some strange things about such a wheel.

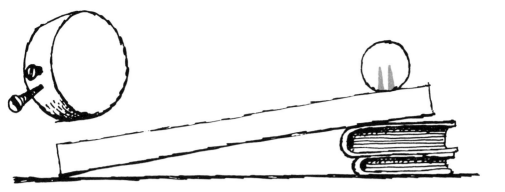

14

How can you make a wheel that will not roll downhill?

Obtain a 3-foot length of wood. Put a book under one end to form a slight hill.

Place a Styrofoam disk at the top of the hill. When you let go of the disk, it rolls down. That is what you would expect it to do.

Next, drive two heavy screws into the middle of the disk's rim. With a screwdriver or a coin, turn the screws until their heads are below the foam. The screws make one part of the wheel heavier than the rest.

With the heavy part at the bottom, put the wheel on the slanting wood again. What does the wheel do this time? It does not roll downhill.

In order to roll downhill, the heavy screws must be lifted. Since the rest of the disk is not heavy enough to lift the screws, the wheel stays where it is. (If the wheel moves, lower the hill until the rolling stops.)

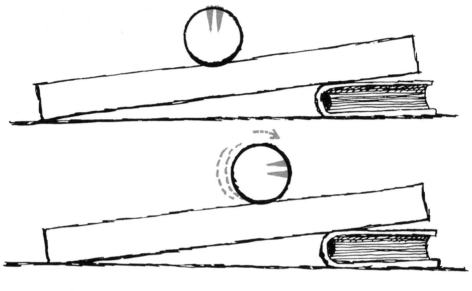

15

You can make a wheel roll uphill.

Set up the length of wood as you did in experiment 14. At the middle of the hill put down the disk with the weighted part on top as shown.

Release the wheel. Does it roll down? No, it rolls up. Gravity pulls the heavier part of the wheel down. In falling, however, the weight makes the wheel itself roll up. If the wheel does not move up, lower the hill until the rolling begins.

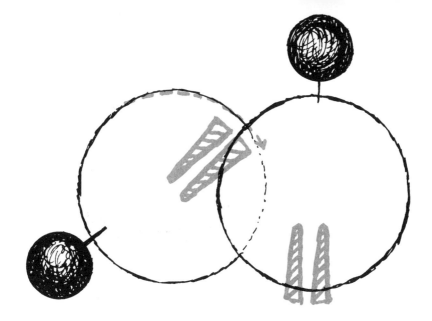

16

A roly-poly is a figure that can be put down but that does not stay down. How does a roly-poly work?

Drive two screws into a large Styrofoam ball. Make sure their heads sink into the foam. With a piece of toothpick, attach a small Styrofoam ball to the large one on the side opposite the screws.

Push the head (small ball) of the roly-poly down to the table. What happens when you let go of the head? It pops right up again.

The reason that it does so is that any downward movement of the head lifts the weight in the large ball. As soon as the head is released, the weight falls and straightens up the roly-poly.

39

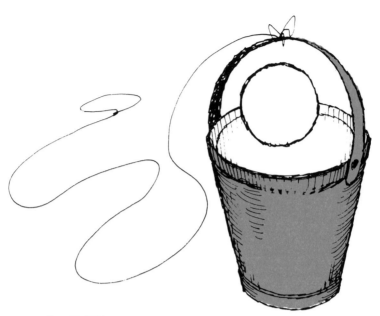

17

How can you turn a pail upside down without having what is inside fall out?

Tie a 2-foot piece of string to the handle of the pail. Put a small foam ball in the pail.

If you just turn the pail upside down, the ball falls out. But if you whirl the pail on the string, the balls stays inside —even when the pail is upside down. Make sure that you whirl the pail in a room where it will not bang into anything.

The ball is forced against the bottom of the pail by the whirling. Gravity is pulling the ball toward the ground as usual, but the effect caused by the whirling balances the force of gravity and keeps the ball from falling out of the pail.

18 A whirling object will move up against the pull of gravity.

Obtain 8 inches of stiff wire and bend it into the shape shown in the picture. Place a large wooden bead on the wire. With the handle, spin the wire loop faster and faster. What happens to the wooden bead?

The bead moves up the wire against the pull of gravity because the effect of the whirling motion is greater than the force of gravity.

What happens to the bead when you stop twirling the wire? Gravity pulls the bead down again.

When the wire is spinning at the right speed, the bead will remain at one level—not moving up and not falling down. When this happens the bead is weightless. This is also what happens to an astronaut when his capsule is in orbit around the earth.

19 Although it is possible to get away from the earth itself, it is quite another matter to escape the earth's gravitational pull. It is this problem that scientists are working to solve in order to be able to send spaceships to explore other planets.

The force of gravity reaches out some 240,000 miles into space, and keeps the moon in orbit around the earth. The earth tugs on the moon, and the moon tugs back on the earth.

Similarly, the sun's gravity holds the earth in orbit. Because the earth pulls back on the sun just as hard as the sun pulls on the earth, the earth's gravity extends about 93,-000,000 miles to the sun.

You have seen that there are ways to balance the earth's pull of gravity, or even overcome it for a short time. Let us now see how scientists use what they know about gravity to put a satellite into orbit around the earth.

Why can't a satellite be launched successfully by a one-stage rocket fired directly from the surface of the earth? Why is it necessary to use a vehicle with two or more rocket stages to put a satellite into orbit?

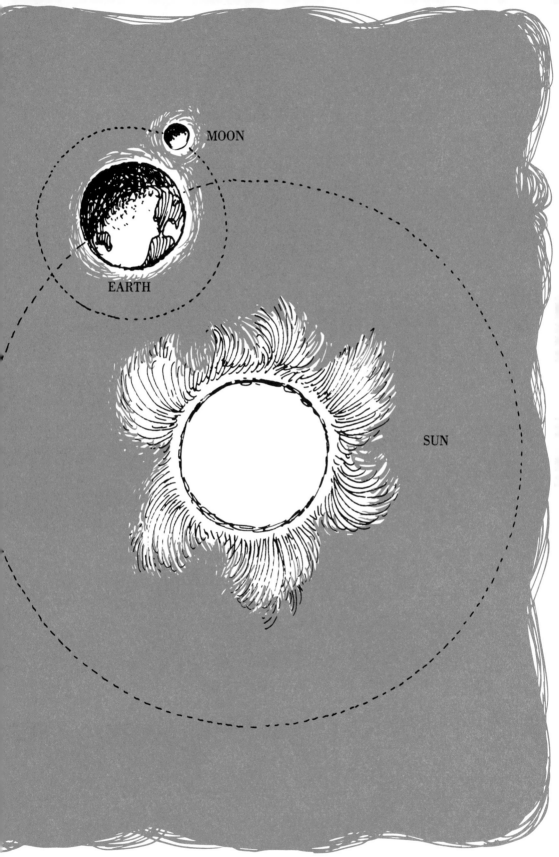

A good way to find the answers to these questions is to build and experiment with a model satellite launcher.

File one end of a 1-foot length of clothes-hanger wire to a point. Insert the other end of the wire into the air hole of a basketball. Tie one end of an 18-inch string to the pointed metal or plastic cap. Attach the lead sinker to the other end of the string. Place the cap on the pointed tip of the wire.

The basketball represents the earth, and the sinker represents the satellite. All that it takes to set the sinker into motion in any direction is a tap of the finger. Let us find out what happens when the satellite is launched in the following ways:

46

1. With a slight tap, push the sinker up and away from the surface of the ball.

The sinker moves up and then falls right back to the starting point. This is how an object travels when it is projected at low speed straight up from the earth.

2. With a slight tap, push the sinker off the surface of the ball at an angle.

The sinker moves away from the ball and then falls back at some distance from the starting point. The distance spanned depends upon the angle of launching and upon the forcefulness of the tap.

47

3. With a stronger tap, push the sinker off the surface of the ball at an angle.

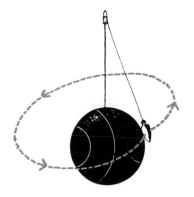

The sinker moves away from the ball, circles it, and lands back at the starting point. To complete its orbit, the sinker must return to the place from which it was launched. A satellite launched in one stage directly from the earth must return to the earth in the same way.

4. With one tap (first stage) push the sinker up from the surface of the ball, and with another tap (second stage) push the sinker in a direction parallel to the surface.

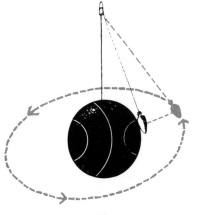

The sinker goes into orbit, circling the ball without touching it. Now, since the starting point of the orbit is off the surface, the orbit is entirely in space, and makes no contact with the ball at any point. The first stage carries the satellite far away from the earth. The other stage puts the vehicle into orbit.

20 The force of gravity becomes weaker as the distance from the earth increases. If a space vehicle arrives at a position where the gravitational attraction of a second body, such as the sun, the moon, or a planet, is stronger than that of the earth, then the ship may become a satellite of the second body, plunge into it, or have its course altered by gravitational effect.

To see how this happens, stretch a sheet of plastic material tightly across the opening of a box, as shown in the diagram. Keep the plastic in place by taping it to the sides. Set a lead sinker down at the center of the plastic sheet. The weight will make the stretched material sag in the middle. Place marbles at the four edges of the box. The marbles will roll from any edge to the center just as if the sinker exerted a gravitational pull on them. In this model, the sinker represents the planetary body and the marbles are the space vehicles.

Fold a 1″ by 12″ strip of heavy cardboard along its length to form the launcher for the marble space vehicle. Tape one end of the launcher to one side of the box. Leave the other end free to move. Launch the marbles by letting them roll down from the free end of the launching runway.

Shift the launcher from one side to the other to control the starting direction of the marble's path. To increase the speed of the marble, raise the free end. Lower it to decrease the speed.

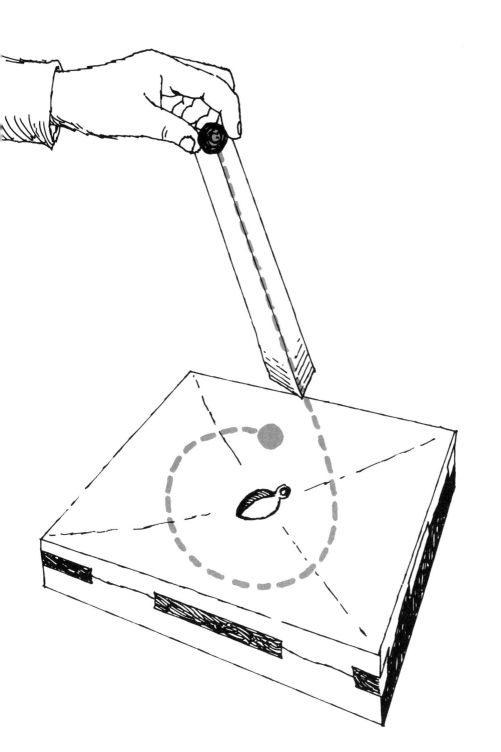

With practice you can arrange the launching runway to make a marble move along one of the three paths a spaceship might follow. At low speed the marble will "land" on the lead sinker "planet."

At higher speed, the marble will spiral around the sinker and become its satellite, or it may spiral closer and closer until it hits the surface of the sinker.

At still higher speed, the marble's path will be bent by the sinker's "pull of gravity." In this case the marble will continue on its way past the target with some change in its direction of travel.

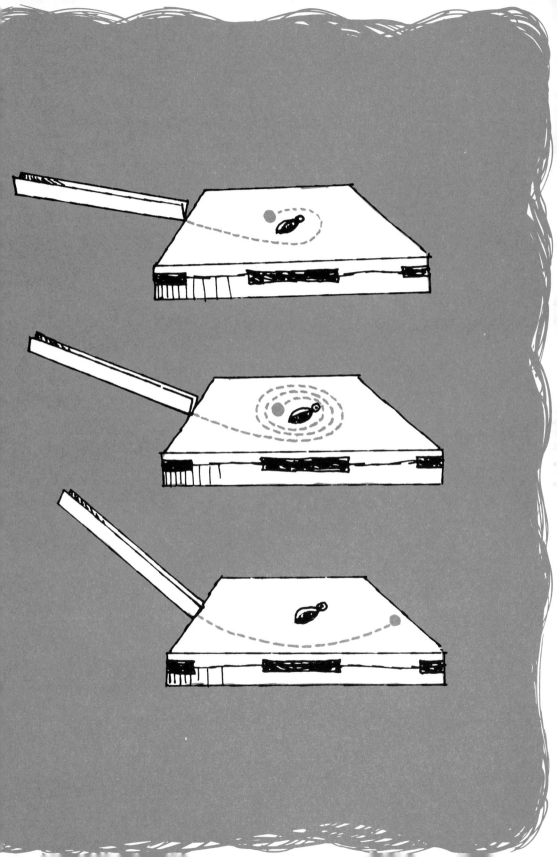

The last experiment showed how the gravitational pull of a planet can change the path of a spaceship traveling at high speed. A planet's tug can also cause the ship to move faster.

Scientists are planning to use the gravitational pull of Venus to speed up the journey from Earth to Mars and back again. The space ship will be launched to travel past Venus. Venus will tug on the ship, change its direction of flight and hurl it at a faster speed towards Mars.

Without the help of Venus the trip to Mars and back might require eight hundred to nine hundred days of travel time. However, the gravitational pull of Venus will increase the speed of the ship so that the round trip will take about 450 days. By reducing the time by a year or so, it will be much easier and safer for astronauts to travel the long road to Mars and back. The picture on the next page illustrates the principle of the Venus bypass to Mars.

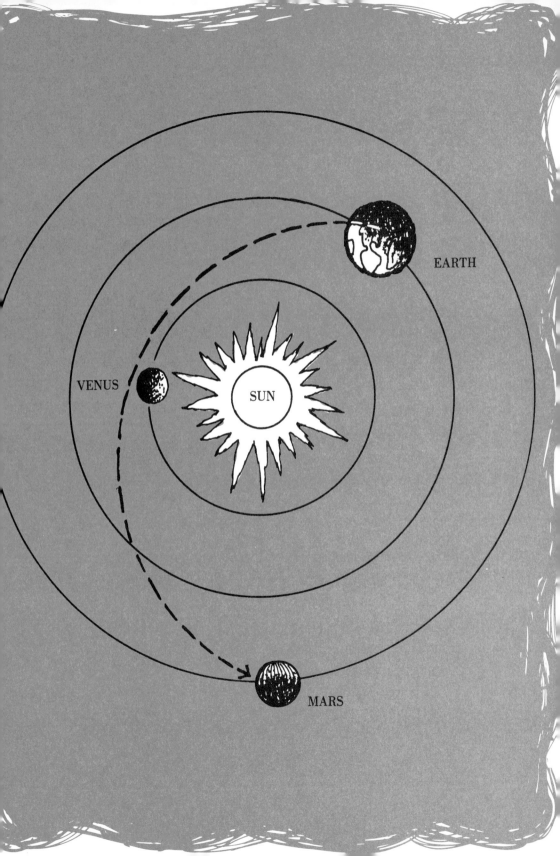

Glossary

AIR RESISTANCE: The force of air against a moving object.

FORCE: A push or a pull that moves or tends to move an object.

FRICTION: The force of resistance to motion between two objects that rub against each other.

GRAVITY (EARTH): The name Sir Isaac Newton gave to the force that pulls objects on or near the surface of the earth toward the earth's center.

ORBIT: The path of an object that revolves around another object.

PENDULUM: A swinging weight.

PLUMB BOB: The weight on the end of a plumb line.

PLUMB LINE: A line or cord with a weight on one end, used to accurately determine up and down.

SATELLITE: An object that is in orbit around a larger object.

SCALE: An instrument with which the amount of the pull of gravity on an object is measured.

WEIGHT (EARTH): The measure of the force of gravity between the matter in an object and the matter in the earth.

WEIGHTLESSNESS: The state of being without weight. This occurs when the earth's force of gravity on an object is balanced by an equal force in the opposite direction; or, when the object is so far from the earth that the force of gravity on it is almost zero.